Aboriginal Legends of Canada

Haida

Megan Cuthbert

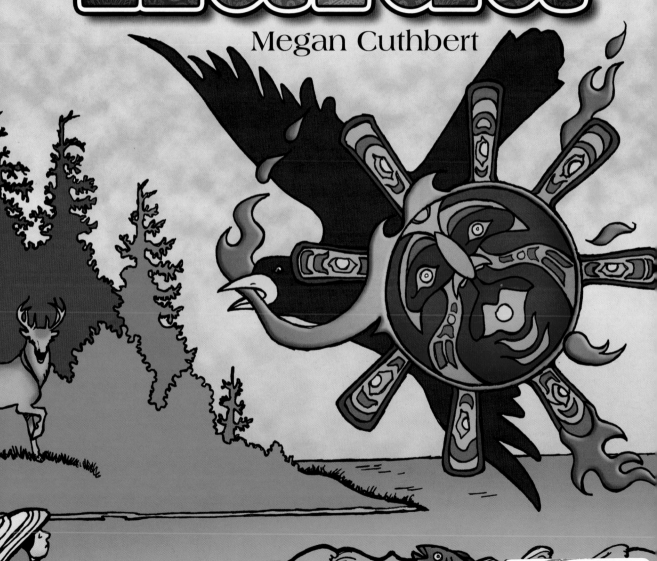

Weigl

Published by Weigl Educational Publishers Limited
6325 10th Street SE
Calgary, Alberta T2H 2Z9

Website: www.weigl.ca

Library and Archives Canada Cataloguing in Publication available upon request.
Fax 403-233-7769 for the attention of the Publishing Records Department.

ISBN 978-1-77071-563-9 (hardcover)
ISBN 978-1-77071-564-6 (softcover)
ISBN 978-1-77071-565-3 (multi-user eBook)

Printed in the United States of America in North Mankato, Minnesota
1 2 3 4 5 6 7 8 9 0 17 16 15 14 13

072013
WEP130613

Project Coordinator: Heather Kissock
Editor: Alexis Roumanis
Design: Mandy Christiansen
Illustrator: Martha Jablonski-Jones

Photo Credits
Weigl acknowledges Alamy and Getty Images as its primary image suppliers for this title.

We acknowledge the financial support of the Government of Canada through the Canada Book Fund for our publishing activities.

CONTENTS

4   Meet the Haida

6   Stories of Creation

8   The Story of the Raven

10   Nature Stories

12   The Coming of
     the Salmon

14   Life Lessons

16   The Foolish Boy and the Cougar

18   Heroic Tales

20   Nanasimget and the Killer
     Whale King

22   Activity

23   Further Research

24   Key Words/Index

Meet the Haida

T he Haida are one of Canada's **Aboriginal Peoples**. They have lived on the islands of Haida Gwaii, off the coast of British Columbia, for more than 6,000 years. In the past, the Haida lived in **longhouses** that were arranged around the longhouse of the chief. Each Haida village was **independent,** with its own leaders and rules. However, Haida villages would come together frequently for large feasts and ceremonies. The people used these events as a way to connect with each other.

Storytelling was a big part of these celebrations. The Haida used stories as a way to share knowledge. Haida stories explain the Haida way of life and teach important lessons. The Haida tell stories through music, dance, art, and the spoken word.

Stories of Creation

The Haida use stories to explain where they came from and to pass on their beliefs to their children. One of the most important types of story the Haida tell is their creation story. This story describes how the world came to be.

The main character in the Haida creation story is Raven. Raven is a key character in Haida **legends**. He is normally portrayed as a trickster. However, through his adventures, he teaches the Haida how to live a good, fulfilling life.

Many stories tell how Raven brought useful items to the Haida. Raven gave them items such as fresh water, salmon, and the house.

Haida rattles sometimes show Raven carrying the Sun in his beak. The Haida believe that the Sun was brought to them by Raven.

Another way that the Haida tell stories is through totem poles. Ravens are common figures on the poles. They are easily recognized by their long beaks.

The Story of the RAVEN

In the beginning, all the world was connected. There were no divisions between humans, animals, or spirits. The world was in total darkness. Then, one day, the trickster Raven stole the Sun from his grandfather. Raven had special powers, and from the Sun he made the Moon and stars. He divided the night and day, and went about creating lakes and rivers. He filled the streams with fish and the forests with animals.

The first people were born in a clamshell. They remained there because they were afraid to leave their home. Slowly, Raven coaxed the people out from the clamshell so they could join him in the new world. These were the first Haida. Raven gave the people the gift of fire. He then disappeared from Earth, taking with him the power of the spirit world to communicate with the humans.

Nature Stories

The Haida have many stories that describe and explain the **natural world**. Some of these stories provide reasons for the way different animals look and behave. Others explain why certain natural events take place. These nature legends are used as a way for Haida children to learn about the world around them.

The Coming of the Salmon indicates the importance of salmon to the Haida people. As the Haida live along Canada's west coast, they rely on the sea for much of their food. Salmon is one of the most common fish in the area and has long been an important food source for the Haida. The story tells how salmon came to live in the waters of the region.

The Haida built canoes from the many cedar trees in the area. The canoes were used for fishing, travel, and battle.

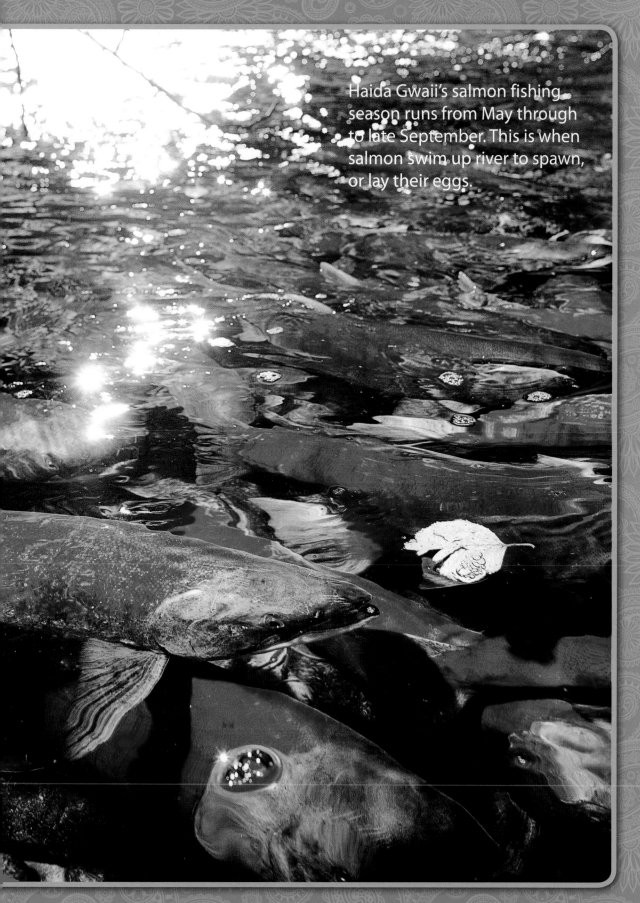

Haida Gwaii's salmon fishing season runs from May through to late September. This is when salmon swim up river to spawn, or lay their eggs.

The COMING of the SALMON

The chief's daughter was crying for a great, shining fish. Her father wanted to find the fish for her, but no one in the village had ever seen a fish like this. Her father called on Raven to help him find the shining fish. Raven assured the chief that he knew the fish well. He promised he would bring the fish to the village.

Raven flew until he saw a group of salmon in the water below him. He swooped down and grabbed a salmon, and headed back to the village. By chance, Raven had caught the son of the Salmon Chief. The Salmon Chief wanted his son back, so he and the other salmon followed Raven.

When Raven brought the salmon to the chief's daughter, she was happy and stopped crying. Raven then told the Haida to set up a net across the river because many more salmon were coming. When the salmon arrived at the village, they were caught in the net. Every year since, the salmon have returned to the waters near the village.

Life Lessons

Some Haida stories are meant to teach lessons about how to behave. These stories are often told to children. They teach the children about right and wrong in a fun and entertaining way. From these stories, the children learn that trouble comes to people who do not behave properly.

Haida artwork, such as jewellery, masks, and sculptures, are another way for the Haida to tell stories. Haida artists often include the creatures and heroes of **traditional** stories in their artwork.

The Foolish Boy and the Cougar tells the story of a young boy who pays a price for refusing to listen to his father. Haida children are taught at an early age to respect their parents and the Haida **elders**. These people are considered to be wise and to have knowledge that young people do not. Children are encouraged to seek guidance from their parents and the elders, and to follow the advice they give.

In recent years, the Haida community has been working closely with its elders to save the Haida language. There are very few speakers left, and most are seniors.

Elders share their knowledge of Haida culture with Haida youth. This ensures that Haida dance, music, and stories are not lost.

The FOOLISH BOY and the COUGAR

A young boy named Sqwally went hunting with his father. When they came to a fork in the path, each decided to take a different part of the path. Before they separated, Sqwally's father warned Sqwally not to go to the Forbidden Forest.

Sqwally wanted to impress his father, who was a great hunter. He decided that he would go to the Forbidden Forest to try to hunt the Great Cougar. He headed toward the forest his father had told him not to enter.

Sqwally was walking through the Forbidden Forest when he heard rustling in the bushes. Before he could throw his spear, the Great Cougar pounced on him.

The Great Cougar had never been seen before. Since Sqwally was the first person to ever see him, the Great Cougar decided not to kill the boy. Instead, he turned Sqwally into a cougar. Once he became a cougar, Sqwally was never able to see his family again.

Heroic Tales

To the Haida, one of the most admirable **traits** a person can have is courage. Many Haida stories tell the tales of heroes, who take remarkable steps to help people and conquer enemies. These stories show how a hero uses **intelligence** and skill to overcome obstacles. Sometimes, these legends are about strong warriors. Others are about everyday people who did the right thing. The heroes of these stories display qualities that the Haida admire.

Nanasimget and the Killer Whale King tells the story of a man who rescues his wife from the Killer Whale King. In doing so, he displays **loyalty** and intelligence. The Haida consider the killer whale to be the most powerful animal in the ocean. Only someone with heroic traits would be able to outwit such a strong animal.

Haida legend says that the first orca was carved from a cedar tree. Today, the orca is featured in the artwork of many Haida artists.

The Haida believe that orcas are very similar to humans. While humans have villages on land, orcas are believed to have underwater communities.

NANASIMGET and the KILLER WHALE KING

After a day of hunting, Nanasimget returned home to his wife with the skin of a white sea otter. His wife was pleased with her present, but it was a bit dirty and needed to be cleaned. When she went into the water to rinse the fur, a great killer whale jumped out of the water and grabbed her. It then dove back into the water, taking Nanasimget's wife with it.

Nanasimget jumped into the water and began swimming after his wife. He encountered many creatures along the way. They told him that the whale that took his wife was the Killer Whale King and that the king wanted to marry Nanasimget's wife.

Nanasimget made a plan with one of the king's slaves. The slave entered the home of the Killer Whale King and poured water on the fire. Smoke filled the room, and Nanasimget was able to enter the house unseen. He rescued his wife, and the two swam back to their village.

Activity

Make a Paper Raven

Raven is the main character in several Haida legends. You can create your own raven using paper.

You Will Need:

round object to
trace around

glue

black and yellow
construction paper

scissors

2 wiggly eyes

1. Using your round object, trace two separate circles onto your black paper, and cut them out with scissors.

2. Cut one of the circles in half.

3. Glue the two half circles onto the main circle to make the raven's wings.

4. Using the yellow paper, cut out a triangle for a beak and two long strips for feet.

5. Glue the beak and legs onto the raven's body.

6. To finish your raven, glue on the two wiggly eyes above the beak.

Further Research

Many books and websites provide information on Aboriginal legends. To learn more about this topic, borrow books from the library, or search the internet.

Books

Most libraries have computers that connect to a database for researching information. If you input a key word, you will be provided with a list of books in the library that contain information on that topic. Nonfiction books are arranged numerically, using their call number. Fiction books are organized alphabetically by the author's last name.

Websites

Watch videos of more Haida legends at :
http://www.haidanation.ca/Pages/ Haida_Legends/Haida_Legends.html

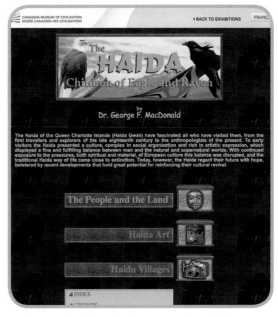

To read about the Haida of the Haida Gwaii, visit:
http://www.civilization.ca/ cmc/exhibitions/aborig/haida/ haindexe.shtml

Key Words

Aboriginal Peoples: First Nations, Inuit, and Métis of Canada

elders: the wise people of a community

independent: does not rely on others

intelligence: the ability to think, learn, and understand

legends: stories that have been passed down from generation to generation

longhouses: rectangular buildings made from cedar

loyalty: strong and lasting support

natural world: relating to things that have not been made by people

traditional: related to established beliefs or practices

traits: qualities or characteristics

Index

art 4, 14, 18

elders 14, 15

Haida Gwaii 4, 23

Raven 6, 7, 8, 12, 13, 22

salmon 6, 10, 11, 12, 13